HANDBOOK
ON RECEIVING THE
HOLY
GHOST

HANDBOOK
ON RECEIVING THE
HOLY
GHOST

FRED E. KINZIE

Handbook on Receiving the Holy Ghost

by Fred E. Kinzie

©Copyright 1997, Word Aflame Press
Hazelwood, MO 63042-2299
Reprint History: 1999

ISBN 1-56722-205-6

Cover design by Paul Povolni
Cover art by Bob Watkins

All Scripture quotations in this book are from the King James Version of the Bible unless otherwise identified.

Printed in United States of America

WORD AFLAME®PRESS
8855 DUNN ROAD
HAZELWOOD, MO 63042-2299

Library of Congress Cataloging-in-Publication Data

Kinzie, Frederick E., 1914–
    Handbook on receiving the Holy Ghost / Fred E. Kinzie.
      p.   cm.
    ISBN 1-56722-205-6
    1. Glossolalia—Handbooks, manuals, etc. 2. Oneness Pentecostal churches—Doctrines—Handbooks, manuals, etc.   I. Title.
BT122.5.K56   1997
234'.13—dc21   97-34869
                                              CIP

To my many mentors, leaders, pastors, evangelists, associates, and friends, both laymen and ministers, who have made invaluable contributions to my sixty years of walking with the Lord Jesus Christ and fifty-five years as a minister of His gospel.

Without these helpful men and women I would be bereft of profound, spiritual insight into the riches of His grace. But with them I have been enriched without measure in the things of God!

Thank God for every one of them!

Contents

Preface

Some time ago I found the manuscript of this booklet in my files. With the exception of the last two chapters, it was written during a time of great revival in the early 1970s at the First Apostolic Church of Toledo, Ohio. Upon discovering it, I decided to print it in its present form. It needed a finishing touch, so I added the last two chapters.

The subject is important to a hungering heart. My desire is to help anyone who is reaching for fulfillment in God.

You will not read the New Testament long before discovering the baptism of the Holy Ghost. It is mentioned in the Gospels, but the Book of Acts assigns it a prominent place. It is definitely a significant part of the salvation experience, so much so that Jesus told Nicodemus he could not enter the kingdom of God without it (John 3:5).

Since it is so important, every believer should seek the gift of the Holy Ghost with his whole heart. As pointed out in this booklet, *seeking* is much more than praying at an altar. It begins with heeding the exhortation of the Bible until a person is thoroughly convinced of its scriptural authority and decides to turn away from his sins. At that point it is a matter of yielding to sincere prayer and praise until Jesus comes in the Spirit to fill the person. Praise is the expressive language of faith, and faith is necessary to receive the Spirit.

Jesus exhorted, "Tarry ye in the city of Jerusalem until ye be endued with power from on high" (Luke 24:49). If He would not allow His disciples to leave Jerusalem without the endowment of the Spirit, then clearly He considered this experience to be of tremendous importance.

To *tarry* means to "wait, pause, stay, delay, remain, or abide." In other words one is to stay his course until he receives the gift of the Holy Ghost. It must become the number-one priority of his life. He must stop, wait, pause, and not occupy himself with any other business until it occurs!

This booklet comes your way in an endeavor to help you receive the Spirit. Don't stop tarrying until!

Introduction

Perhaps no area of the Word of God has been more neglected or misunderstood than the Spirit's action in the birth of a true Christian and the person's maintenance of that new life in the Spirit.

A handbook of pertinent instructions for receiving the Spirit has been long overdue. We are often guilty of expecting the unsaved to understand God's plan for their lives upon bending their knees at our altars. But frankly, no one comes to this knowledge without instruction. Frequently it is a long wait as the penitent slowly grasps truth from a variety of sources. Often what he hears is a mixture of faith and law from unskilled or uninstructed sources, and consequently a conglomeration of ideas emerges that hinders rather than helps him come to the saving knowledge of God.

After sixty years in the Christian life and seeing multitudes receive the Holy Ghost, I desire to bring hungry hearts to that wonderful pinnacle of Christian experience, the reception of the gift of the Holy Ghost. With this thought in mind, I urge those who read this brief treatise to follow the Bible references and take ample time in prayer and meditation to facilitate its fulfillment in their lives.

The Christian life is exciting and power packed. God intended it to be that way, and those who have not yet discovered this fact are living far beneath God's promise. May God hasten the moment that you believe His promise and enter into God's fullness for your life.

Faith launches us on a venture that ends in heaven as a member of the church of the Lord Jesus Christ, His bride. The promise of the Holy Ghost is to every believer in Christ and is the seal of our faith in Him, providing the explicit knowledge whereby we know that Christ abides in our hearts. (See Ephesians 1:13-14; II Corinthians 1:22; I John 3:24; 4:13; 5:6.) It is heaven's witness to us, and our experience in God is incomplete without it. (See John 3:8.)

It is for this very reason that each of us should seek the Holy Ghost baptism. Seeking is more than praying at an altar, although it includes prayer. Seeking takes into account the validity of this experience with God. Is it scriptural? Does the Word of God teach that we can and must receive the Holy Ghost? Only as we understand that it is scriptural and that God expects everyone to receive the Holy Ghost, will we receive. Hebrews 11:6 proclaims, "Without faith it is impossible to please him, for he that cometh to God must believe that he is, and that he is a rewarder of them that diligently seek him."

So it is correct to seek the Lord diligently through the Word and prayer. And so, first of all, let us seek the scriptural authority for receiving the Holy Ghost.

CHAPTER ONE

Scriptural Authority

Although the baptism of the Holy Ghost was veiled in a variety of utterances in Old Testament times, it was John the Baptist who introduced it to the world of the New Testament. John came for the specific purpose of making people aware that Jesus had come. His was the voice in the wilderness trumpeting forth that Jesus was here. One must not miss the impact of his introduction of the Son, Jesus Christ. He not only said, "Here He is," but he also introduced what He came to do. (See Isaiah 40:3; John 1:6-9, 23, 29, 33.)

John's Introduction

"Behold the Lamb of God, which taketh away the sin of the world" (John 1:29) were the words John used to call the attention of the world to the Lord Jesus Christ. He did not stop with this utterance, however. It represented but half of what Jesus came to do. Half the truth is good—if it is not meant to deceive. But God wants everyone to know the whole truth. (See I Timothy 2:4.)

The Baptist followed his first words of introduction with a significant statement: "I indeed baptize you with water; but one mightier than I cometh, the latchet of whose shoes I am not worthy to unloose; he shall baptize you with the Holy Ghost and with fire" (Luke 3:16). While only the Gospel of John records the statement, "Behold the Lamb of God," each of the four evangelists records this second part of John the Baptist's introduction. (See Matthew 3:11; Mark 1:8; Luke 3:16; John 1:33.) Their treatment does not mean that the first statement of John the Baptist is only one-fourth true, but it does mean that while the first part is true, the second receives four times as much emphasis. If Jesus Christ came to deal with the sin problem (which He did at Calvary, see Romans 5:10), even more so He came to impart His life to those whose sins are cleansed. To clean up the house but leave it unoccupied invites disaster. (See Luke 11:24-26.)

"I indeed baptize you with water; but one mightier than I cometh, the latchet of whose shoes I am not worthy to unloose" (Luke 1:33).

The life and ministry of Jesus was not limited to these two things. No life on earth was so filled with activity, so meaningful, so power packed, so important as His. Indeed John recorded, "There are also many other things which Jesus did, the which, if they should be written every one, I suppose that even the world itself could not contain the books that should be written" (John 21:25).

Among the many other things Jesus said and did, the two things just listed are paramount. They form the main thrust of His coming into the world. All other things, though important, are secondary. We must never lose sight of these two weighty matters, for in the end everything will revolve around them. They represent the heart of creation, the eternal purpose of God, the reason all things exist. If we miss them we have missed everything; if we find them we embrace the whole handiwork of God in eternity past, present, and future. (See Colossians 1:14, 16-17; Ephesians 1:9-10; 2:7, 10.)

Obviously, our subject is no passing fancy, no Johnny-come-lately affair. When we participate in it, we become involved with the heartbeat of God! Whatever we do, we must not take it lightly. (See Romans 8:18-24; 11:33-36; Hebrews 12:25-29.)

As strange as it may seem, in the early ministry of Christ He was almost silent on the subject of the baptism of the Holy Ghost. It was as though He was unaware of what John had said. Not so! He simply put first things first. He first had to fulfill His mission as the Messiah, the King of Israel who would reestablish the kingdom with Himself on the throne of David. (See Luke 19:35-44.) But Israel did not receive Him because they were blinded as to who He was. (See Romans 11:7-10.) Because of the promise of God, however, they had priority (Romans 1:16). John declared, "He came unto his own, and his own received him not" (John 1:11).

As a nation, the Jews rejected Jesus by demanding His crucifixion. (See I Corinthians 2:7, 8; Luke 23:13-25.) This choice did not thwart God's ultimate plan; instead He used it as a means of launching His mission to the entire world. The apostle Paul stated, "The diminishing of them [was] the riches of the Gentiles" (Romans 11:12).

Israel's rejection thrust upon the world the heart of God's divine purpose. He established His church, composed of both Jews and Gentiles, which in other ages had been hidden from the understanding of the prophets. (See Ephesians 2:11-12; 3:4-9.)

Jesus' Last Days

John's Gospel recounts the last days of Jesus in the greatest detail. John 13-18 is the record of the last night before His crucifixion. It is here that the most intimate of Jesus' conversations with His apostles took place. On His last night, He spoke to them in depth for the first time about the role of the Spirit, both in the purpose of God and in their personal lives. In John 14:16 the subject of the Spirit's operation comes to the forefront. He spoke of another Comforter who dwelt with them and would soon be in them. He then revealed that He Himself would actually be that Comforter in Spirit form. (See John 14:16-18.)

At this point Jesus began preparing them for a new relationship with God. His manifestation in the flesh would be withdrawn from their presence and His spiritual relationship with them would replace it. In this spiritual relationship they would experience the fullness, the completeness, of God's divine purpose for them. (See John

14:2, 12, 21; Ephesians 1:10; Colossians 2:9-10.)

Other References by Jesus

The Bible records references of Jesus to this new relationship even before the last night with His disciples. In Luke, at the conclusion of His answer to the disciples' question about prayer, He affirmed the willingness of God to respond to simple faith and prayer. He assured them that God would not deceive them or substitute the false for the true but would give the Holy Spirit to those who asked Him. Jesus further extolled the virtue of persistence as an integral element of sincere supplication to the Lord. (See Luke 11:1, 8-13; 18:5.)

"Jesus stood and cried, saying, If any man thirst, let him come unto me, and drink" (John 7:37).

A second reference came in an invitation Jesus gave at the Feast of Tabernacles as He viewed the milling throng searching for an answer to their spiritual thirst. In parentheses, John, sixty years later, correctly interpreted the statement Jesus made that day. Here is the statement with John's interpretation:

"Jesus stood and cried, saying, If any man thirst, let him come unto me, and drink. He that believeth on me, as the scripture hath said, out of his belly shall flow rivers of living water. (But this spake he of the Spirit, which they that believe on him should receive: for the Holy Ghost was not yet given; because that Jesus was not yet glorified)" (John 7:37-39).

In his explanation John insisted that every genuine believer should be a receiver.

These two references form additional links in the chain of scriptural authority for receiving the Holy Ghost as an integral part of the salvation experience.

The Post-resurrection Ministry of Jesus

After His resurrection Jesus placed marked emphasis upon a person's receiving the Holy Ghost. He now set about the task of preparing His disciples for the experience that would seal them as His and empower them to accomplish His purpose in and through them. He commanded them to receive the Holy Ghost. (See Acts 1:4-8; John 20:22; Luke 24:49; II Timothy 2:19; II Corinthians 1:21-22.)

Luke and John recorded the most pertinent information concerning this truth. John gave the account of Jesus coming to His disciples after His resurrection and commissioning them to their future task. Then Jesus breathed on them and commanded them to receive the Holy Ghost. They did not receive the Spirit at that moment or on that day, for according to Acts it was at least ten days later that they received. It was mandatory, however, that they receive, not optional as some claim today.

From other passages of Scripture we learn that it is imperative for all who would be saved in the New

Testament church. Some teach that only twelve received the Holy Ghost at Pentecost, but Scripture contradicts this view. (See John 20:19-23; Luke 24:49; Acts 2:1-4, 38-39; 8:14-17; 10:43-48; Galatians 3:2.)

Jesus commanded His followers to receive the Holy Ghost. Only afterwards can they effectively carry out their assigned task of preaching the gospel and offering remission of sins to those who come to Christ seeking forgiveness. (See John 20:22-23; Acts 1:8.) If they do not have the experience of the Holy Ghost, how can they preach it to others? As we will see later, remission of sins is accomplished through repentance and water baptism in the name of Jesus Christ. (See Acts 2:38; 22:16.)

Luke noted that Jesus miraculously opened the understanding of His disciples (Luke 24:49). He turned on the light of illumination within them. He will do the same for anyone today who will seek Him sincerely and honestly.

Pentecost

Up until now we have been dealing mostly with this subject before the Day of Pentecost. Now we come face to face with Pentecost, the birthday of God's magnificent church. (See Acts 2:1-42.)

Pentecost, for the Jews, was a feast commemorating the giving of the law to Israel. We find the true Pentecost, however, which the giving of the law foreshadowed, in the second chapter of Acts. The outpouring of the Holy Ghost signaled, according to Paul, the writing of the nature of God, not on tables of stone, but on the fleshly tables of the heart. The giving of the law on stone pointed forward

19

to the divine nature being embodied in flesh. The church is that embodiment of God through the Spirit. (See Acts 2; Exodus 19:10; 23:16; 34:22; Leviticus 23:16; II Corinthians 3:3; II Peter 1:4; Ephesians 2:21-22.)

On the Day of Pentecost, God inhabited His new temple, the church. This temple had been prepared by His instructions during His tenure on earth, especially His last day before death and during the forty days after His resurrection. The preparations involved His death, burial, and resurrection, without which no one would have received the Spirit at Pentecost. (See I Corinthians 3:16; John 13-18; Acts 1:1-8; Romans 5:10.)

Pentecost is always prefaced by preparation. Prior to the giving of the law, certain preparation requirements were issued. We will deal with them, as pertaining to our Pentecost, in the next chapter. (See Exodus 19:10-15.)

"Men and brethren, what shall we do?" (Acts 2:37).

Pentecost came—a sound as of a rushing mighty wind filled the house, cloven tongues like fire appeared and sat upon each person, and everyone began speaking in other tongues. This action was divine. It came from God out of heaven. It necessitated believers being at the right place, at the right time, and with the proper attitude. (See Acts 2:1.) No individual could have stopped this outpouring of the Holy Ghost any more than someone could have started it. The main thing the disciples had to do was be present.

Two things happened on that day that never happened again in Scripture (Acts 2:2-3):

    1. The sound as of a mighty rushing wind

    2. The appearance of tongues like fire

Two other things occurred that would occur again (Acts 2:4, 7, 12-13):

    1. Speaking in other tongues as the Spirit gave utterance

    2. The amazement of those who witnessed it, with reactions both pro and con

Peter preached the first message after this experience on Pentecost. Closing his message, he proclaimed the promise of the Holy Ghost. Those who heard him preach asked, "Men and brethren, what shall we do?" (Acts 2:37). He answered:

"Repent, and be baptized every one of you in the name of Jesus Christ for the remission of sins, and ye shall receive the gift of the Holy Ghost. For the promise is unto you, and unto your children, and to all that are afar off, even as many as the Lord our God shall call" (Acts 2:38-39).

This promise includes every one of us!

Peter's answer formed the foundation for faith that entitles us to receive! Paul affirmed in Ephesians 2:13 that the Gentiles were once afar off but have now been brought near by the blood of Christ. Peter proclaimed that the promise is to "as many as the Lord our God shall call" (Acts 2:39), which certainly embraces each of us. The only qualification to fit us into this promise is the assurance in our own hearts that God is dealing with us, calling us to Himself. If He is, then this promise belongs to us. Let us believe it!

After Pentecost

Five accounts in the Book of Acts describe believers receiving the Holy Ghost. (See Acts 2:1-12; 8:16-17; 9:17; 10:44-48; 19:1-6.) We must not be misled by those who intimate that the other incidents of salvation in Acts were devoid of this experience. Because all of the essential factors of salvation are not cited on each occasion does not mean they did not happen. It would be pure folly and biblically inconsistent to maintain that silence suggests they did not occur. The same would also be true about water baptism in the name of Jesus Christ.

For instance, let us take the case of Paul. On three occasions the Book of Acts cites his salvation experience. One account omits water baptism, but the other two state he was baptized. The same is true about the three accounts of the first Gentiles to enter the church. One states that they were baptized; the other two are silent. It would be ridiculous to assume that because baptism is not mentioned in all these accounts it did not happen. Again it would be unreasonable to maintain the same about faith, repentance, and receiving the Holy Ghost. Every salvation experience had all factors to be acceptable in the sight of God.

We must not be misled by someone who attempts to discredit the record in Acts. It is the book of salvation experiences in the early church. Without it we would not have the following:
- a record of the outpouring of the Holy Ghost
- a record of the beginning of the church
- a record of the salvation experience of Paul
- a record of the Gentiles being saved
- a record of the spread of the church in the world

Without the record of Acts, we would be a lost community, unable to determine where we fit into the program of God! If there are different ways and requirements for salvation in the Book of Acts, then God is guilty of partiality. Peter, when speaking to the household of Cornelius, declared God to be impartial. (See Acts 2:38; 3:19; 4:4; 5:14; 8:12, 16; 10:34; 19:5; 26:20.) For a more thorough discussion of this subject see Fred Kinzie, *Salvation in the Book of Acts*, page 88.

"And God, which knoweth the hearts, bare them witness, giving them the Holy Ghost, even as he did unto us" (Acts 15:8).

We should note two further verses in Acts that substantiate the divine origin of the gift of the Holy Ghost and the expectation that every believer should receive it. Acts 5:32 states, "And we are witnesses of these things;

and so is also the Holy Ghost, whom God hath given to them that obey him." Then Acts 15:8 says, "And God, which knoweth the hearts, bare them witness, giving them the Holy Ghost, even as he did unto us."

The book is entitled Acts because it records the action of the Holy Ghost in and through people whom God chose to be His vessels. The Book of Acts proclaims that receiving the Holy Ghost is a definite, knowable, divine experience—so much so that one can categorically answer yes or no to the question Paul posed to the Ephesians: "Have ye received the Holy Ghost since ye believed?" (Acts 19:2).

"Have ye received the Holy Ghost since ye believed?" (Acts 19:2).

The Epistles

As in the Gospels and Acts, there are several references to receiving the Holy Ghost in the Epistles. Beginning with Romans 8, we find many verses that teach us to know and experience the Spirit baptism. Eighteen times this chapter mentions or alludes to the Spirit. Romans 8:16 says the Spirit will witness to our sonship. "How will the Spirit witness?" one may ask. We find the answer as we study the passages that describe the evidence that accompanied the outpouring of the Spirit in the early church. (See Acts 2:4; 5:32; 10:46; 15:8; 19:6.)

If the Spirit witnesses, the Spirit must have a means of utterance, which Acts 2:4 reveals to be speaking in tongues. The witness is more than a feeling, although feelings may be part of it.

"Received ye the Spirit by the works of the law, or by the hearing of faith?" (Galatians 3:2).

Paul's epistles to the Corinthians contain several references to the operation of the Spirit. Though they do not recount the actual salvation experience, they refer back to it. (See I Corinthians 3:16; 6:11, 19; 12:13; II Corinthians 1:22; 3:3; 5:5.)

In Galatians 3:2 Paul asked a significant question. It is apparent that he knew the Galatians had specific knowledge of the Spirit's operation within them. "This only would I learn of you," he asked, "Received ye the Spirit by the works of the law, or by the hearing of faith?"

The answer is obvious. They knew when they received and also how they received.

Again in this same chapter Paul linked the blessing of Abraham with the promise of the Spirit (Galatians 3:14).

There are many other allusions to receiving the Holy Ghost throughout the rest of the Epistles. Here are some of them:

• "In whom ye also are builded together for an habitation of God through the Spirit. . . . And be not drunk with wine, wherein is excess; but be filled with the Spirit" (Ephesians 2:22; 5:18).

• "Not by works of righteousness which we have done, but according to his mercy he saved us, by the washing of regeneration, and renewing of the Holy Ghost; which he shed on us abundantly through Jesus Christ our Saviour" (Titus 3:5-6).

• "God also bearing them witness, both with signs and wonders, and with divers miracles, and gifts of the Holy Ghost, according to his own will. . . . For it is impossible for those who were once enlightened, and have tasted of the heavenly gift, and were made partakers of the Holy Ghost, and have tasted the good word of God, and the powers of the world to come, if they shall fall away, to renew them again unto repentance; seeing they crucify to themselves the Son of God afresh, and put him to an open shame" (Hebrews 2:4; 6:4-6).

"And it is the Spirit that beareth witness, because the Spirit is truth" (I John 5:6).

• "And he that keepeth his commandments dwelleth in him, and he in him. And hereby we know that he abideth in us, by the Spirit which he hath given us. . . . Hereby know we that we dwell in him, and he in us because he has given us of his Spirit. . . . This is he that came by water and blood, even Jesus Christ; not by water only, but by water and blood. And it is the Spirit that beareth witness, because the Spirit is truth" (I John 3:24; 4:13; 5:6).

These passages should be sufficient to convince a person that receiving the Holy Ghost is an operation of God—and normal for believers. It is true and safe to assume from the Epistles that all believers in the early church received the Holy Ghost.

How much more does one need to believe that receiving the Holy Ghost has adequate scriptural authority? To deny or ignore the Scripture, which leaves no doubt as to the authenticity of receiving the Holy Ghost, would be senseless.

Salvation in the Book of Acts lists thirty-three references to this experience in the New Testament (pages 98-100).

If someone has not yet received the Holy Ghost with the scriptural witness of speaking in other tongues as the Spirit gives utterance, he needs to ask himself why.

There are only two significant barriers: *sin* and *unbelief*. We will deal with them in the next two chapters. If you are honest and hungry, get ready! You will soon be a receiver!

CHAPTER TWO

The Barrier of Sin

In the final analysis, there is only one thing that can keep someone from receiving the Holy Ghost, and that is sin. While unbelief blocks a person, in reality unbelief is sin.

I did not write "sins." If I would have put the word in the plural, the immediate tendency would be to set on a course to discern which of many sins is the culprit. There are many sins, and it would be impossible to list them all. The problem is not just certain acts of sin, however; it is the state of sin, which produces a variety of manifestations. The nature of sin is the basic problem that each of us must deal with in our lives.

Sin began in the Garden of Eden, when Adam and Eve partook of the forbidden fruit. The act of eating was only the effect, not the cause. Any act of sin, regardless of its nature, is the result of something much deeper. What is that deeper cause?

It boils down to two things—and eventually down to one. The two things are disobedience and unbelief.

Actually, the root cause of disobedience is unbelief. Adam and Eve failed to believe that God meant what He said. Their unbelief, although suggested to them by Satan, fostered disobedience to God's command and grew into an act of transgression.

"But of the tree of the knowledge of good and evil, thou shalt not eat of it: for in the day that thou eatest thereof thou shalt surely die" (Genesis 2:17).

God laid down one law and then gave the consequence of not keeping it. It was a *law of refraining.* "And the LORD God commanded the man, saying, Of every tree of the garden thou mayest freely eat: but of the tree of the knowledge of good and evil, thou shalt not eat of it: for in the day that thou eatest thereof thou shalt surely die" (Genesis 2:16-17).

This command was quite simple. But Satan had a way of blinding Adam and Eve to the can-do's and focusing on the can't-do's. A luscious, fruit-filled, beautiful garden lay before them, a paradise of rich, good things, but Satan called their attention to the one thing God told them not to do.

Their disobedience brought sin into the human race, and consequently their response is characteristic of basic human nature today. There is a tendency to skepticism and unbelief in all of us. With this nature of sin resident in us, it is difficult for us to take God at His Word. Even with all the examples in the Bible to the contrary, we still struggle with this basic problem.

When we come to God, most of the time "sins" occupy our approach. We ask God's forgiveness, and when we repent and are baptized in the name of Jesus Christ they are remitted—paid for, charged to the account of Jesus Christ. It is like signing a check to pay a bill. When someone places his name on the bottom right-hand line, he commits the amount of the check to be transferred to the account of the recipient. When we are baptized in the name of Jesus Christ, by that act of obedient faith we commit our sins to His account, an account He paid two thousand years ago. Until we are baptized in the name of Jesus Christ, however, the transfer of sins to His account is no more accomplished than is a debt paid until the check is signed.

So repentance and water baptism take care of our sins (plural). "Sins" refers to our own personal breaking of the law of God. But what about the cause of those sins? Is it still there? Does it still hold the potential to create new situations in which we could become involved in wrong acts once again? Could more sins pile up against us although the former ones are forgiven and remitted?

Romans 6 and 7

These questions bring us to the heart of Paul's teaching to the Romans. The old man with all of his pollution and filth is buried by baptism into the death of Jesus

Christ. Indeed, only in this way can we identify with His death and be "in Him." The rest of Romans 6 and 7 deals not merely with sins but with the basic cause of them, the inherent unbelief that fosters disobedience and erupts into sins. We must deal with, defeat, and overcome this basic nature of sin, not merely by a principle or an act, but by a new life in the Spirit.

One does not have to understand all the fundamental facts of Romans 6 and 7 to receive the Holy Ghost. What happens to most people is that the moving of the Spirit produces an attitude within a truly penitent person that equips him to yield to God. Those who have already received the Holy Ghost before they understood Romans 6 and 7 can attest to this truth. For those who have not received, understanding will help them believe.

If you have not yet received the Holy Ghost, perhaps you do not know what is wrong. You wonder! You pray! You weep! You seek the Lord! "Why don't I receive the Holy Ghost?" you wonder. Thank God for that wonderment. The devil tells you either it is not for you or you have committed the unpardonable sin. When my companion and I were seeking the Lord, Satan almost convinced her that she had committed this sin. Such doubt has a discouraging effect and has caused many to give up in despair. But the passages of Scripture we studied in the first chapter should convince you that the Holy Ghost is for you! That is what Peter preached on the Day of Pentecost. The Lord demonstrated that this gift was for all who believe by baptizing the Samaritans and Gentiles with the Holy Ghost. So this experience *is* for you! (See

Acts 8:12-17; 10:34-48.)

What Is My Trouble?

The stubborn unbelief that we were born with always seems to pop up its ugly head right when it should not. For this reason the apostle Paul, as he reviewed his past struggle, exclaimed, "O wretched man that I am! who shall deliver me from the body of this death?" (Romans 7:24).

"O wretched man that I am! who shall deliver me from the body of this death?" (Romans 7:24).

How wonderful it was when Jesus filled Saul (Paul) with the Holy Ghost and through the law of the Spirit of life in Christ Jesus, took over the lordship of his life. He could not do it himself. When Ananias laid his hands on Paul he received the Holy Ghost and his sight was restored. He was transported from darkness to light, from unbelief to faith, and from death to life. He could now see through the Spirit, not just with natural eyes the light of day but with illuminated spiritual insight into the things of God. No longer was he disobedient to the heavenly vision, but he immediately yielded to it. (See Acts 22:12-16; 26:19.) He certainly did not have an automatic understanding of all of God's plan and purposes—that was to come later by revelation during a three-year sojourn in

Arabia—but he immediately loved the One he once hated. Straightway he began telling others about Him, telling what happened when he encountered Christ.

Perhaps the less ecclesiastically inclined one is, the easier it is to yield to God. Often tradition or one's former teaching presents what seems to be an almost insurmountable barrier. It may make it very difficult to believe. One wants to do right, tries to do right, struggles to do right, but tradition, which wrote off the Holy Ghost experience, gets in the way. To believe seems almost impossible for one who has to leap over the tradition barrier. So often he must undo so much before he can progress. The struggle can be very painful. Although most of the time we do not consider it as such, our unbelief is the hindrance, and all unbelief is sin. What can we do about it?

"Lord, I believe; help thou my unbelief" (Mark 9:24).

Lord, Help My Unbelief

Jesus encountered a man who said, "Lord, I believe; help thou my unbelief" (Mark 9:24). That is a good prayer if it is really sincere. Again it is not merely a matter of particular sins. If it is, then we should repent of those sins. And we reach the real depths of repentance when we cry out like the tax collector, "God, be merciful to me a sinner" (Luke 18:13).

This cry makes us realize that mercy is our only hope.

The mercy of God is clearly demonstrated for us at Calvary. Why would One who should not have died, die for one who should? Only grace and mercy put Him in our place.

"He that is dead is freed from sin" (Romans 6:7).

The essence of Romans 6 and 7 is that we are to yield our members to God (Romans 6:13). As one time we yielded them to sin, so now we are to yield them to God. The reason God could use Paul was that he fervently yielded himself to whatever course he determined. When he served Satan, though he thought he was serving God, he served him fervently. When he turned to God he served Him just as fervently. Paul suggested that with the same intensity we once yielded ourselves to the forces of sin, so now we should yield ourselves to God (Romans 6:19). This is the secret of finding God in the baptism of the Spirit.

We receive the solution to the problem of sins by dying to the law through the death of Jesus Christ. When we are baptized into Christ, we are baptized into His death; we are thereby identified with His death and burial. Paul stated, "He that is dead is freed from sin" (Romans 6:7).

Sin is the transgression of the law, and where there is no law there is no transgression (Romans 4:15). Since we are identified with Christ in His death by baptism, we have no more sins, because where there is no law there is no sin (Romans 4:15). That is what justification means. We are cleared clear in heaven's court, and stand just as though we had never sinned. Yet Paul stated that when he wanted to do good, evil was present (Romans 7:21). Finally, he confessed that it was "sin," the unbelief from which all acts of sin spring, that caused this trouble (Romans 7:23). In Romans 7:24, the "body of this death" is the unbelief that is basic to our nature. But thank God, everything changes when we become a partaker of His nature through the Holy Ghost. (See Romans 7:25; II Peter 1:4.)

"That the righteousness of the law might be fulfilled in us, who walk not after the flesh, but after the Spirit" (Romans 8:4).

Romans 6:1-6 is a statement of truth, and the rest of that chapter and all of chapter 7 illustrate and explain it. Nowhere in chapters 6 and 7 did Paul refer to "sins" (plural) as in Acts 2:38. He wrote about the body of sin, the principle by which we are held captive, inherited from our ancestors and a force that must be destroyed through the resurrection of Christ. When His resurrection life becomes ours—by our receiving the Holy Ghost—we find the deliverance from the old nature of unbelief. It caused us to disobey, and if we quit walking in the Spirit it can take over again—making us carnal and subject to spiritual death (Romans 8:4-6).

The old man, or the nature of sin, is an inclination to unbelief. It fosters disobedience and keeps us from yielding to God.

I faced this problem in the early part of my walk with God. Brought up in a church that did not believe in receiving the Holy Ghost, I doubted when told about it.

Finally, when I gave my heart to God in repentance and was baptized, I was informed that I had received the Holy Ghost even though I was not conscious of a definite experience. Nevertheless, I accepted the word of the minister.

Shortly after I was baptized, a lady told me that God wanted me to receive the Holy Ghost. I looked at her askance, shunning the statement as though she did not know what she was talking about. I thought I had the Holy Ghost, at least that is what the minister had said, and who was she to insult my integrity?

The more I thought and prayed about it, however, the less sure I became. I read tracts on the baptism of the Holy Ghost which taught that speaking in tongues had nothing whatsoever to do with it. Utterly confused, I drifted into a state of frustration in which I did not know where I was. If I had received the Holy Ghost, I did not know where or when, and if Paul questioned me as he did the Ephesians in Acts 19:2, I could not have answered intelligently.

Later I was to learn that it is not difficult to answer if one has received. You will know! No one needs to tell you as the minister did me. I realize now that because of his errant beliefs he was trying to pull me away from what he called the "evidence" people. I followed him for a while until I was practically spiritually bankrupt. A great longing gripped my heart. If that longing for reality had not been satisfied by receiving the Holy Ghost, I believe I would have drifted back and never been saved. But thank God, He opened my understanding when I turned sincerely to His Word, followed its instructions, and waited as the disciples did—praising, blessing, and worshiping God until one morning, when I least expected, God came to me in the Spirit, filled me, and made me to know for certain He was there! (See Luke 24:49-50.)

CHAPTER THREE

When Faith Goes to Work

"I want the Holy Ghost on Easter," she announced to me as she entered the foyer of the church that Sunday evening. There were no misgivings in the tone of her voice. That there was a Holy Ghost baptism, and that it was for her, she affirmed with a confident expression on her face and an assuring intonation in her voice.

She had attended Sunday school for the first time that Sunday morning. Though the lesson was short because of an Easter program, a girlfriend had witnessed to her about redemption through the Cross and the baptism in the Spirit. These words awakened a sincere desire within her heart. All day long the thought of finding Christ, and being filled with the Spirit, had captivated her heart. She believed it was for her. On the way to church she expressed her feeling to her girlfriend. She was assured it could and would happen if she believed.

When she entered the church that evening, she was so eager that she wanted to be baptized immediately. I informed her she could be baptized at the close of the service. She prayed at the altar for a few moments and then came looking for me. "May I be baptized right now?" she asked. She was immediately prepared for baptism. While being instructed about baptism she interrupted several times to exclaim, "I want the Holy Ghost on Easter!" She had firmly fixed this desire in her heart. It was her faith. She believed it was for her and that she would receive.

That she did not receive the Holy Ghost before or when she was baptized surprised me. As she walked down the steps from the baptistery, however, she stopped, lifted her hands towards heaven, and prayed, "Lord, I want the Holy Ghost today—on the day commemorating Your resurrection—and I'm staying right here until I receive." That is exactly what she did. It was not two minutes later that she began speaking in other tongues as the Spirit gave her utterance. God responded to her positive, undoubting faith. He always will!

"Then Peter said unto them, Repent, and be baptized every one of you in the name of Jesus Christ for the remission of sins, and ye shall receive the gift of the Holy Ghost" (Acts 2:38)

As we analyze this account, we can readily recognize some important ingredients of faith. First of all, faith produces a positive attitude. There was not one negative thought in her mind. She did not argue, but rather believed. The expression on her face when she announced to me, "I want the Holy Ghost on Easter," was one of absolute confidence. The service only served to accelerate it. The short prayer at the altar brought further confirmation, and she was ready to obey the Scripture: "Then Peter said unto them, Repent, and be baptized every one of you in the name of Jesus Christ for the remission of sins, and ye shall receive the gift of the Holy Ghost" (Acts 2:38).

Later she told me that the word "repent" that was affixed to the pulpit, and the rest of Acts 2:38 above the baptistery, kept burning in her heart while she sat through the service. She related that the more she read it the greater became the assurance that God's promise would soon be fulfilled in her life. Faith was working, and when faith goes to work things happen.

Not every person's experience is the same. Some grasp truth quickly; others it dawns on gradually. God is the same, but the capacity to appropriate God's promises differs with individuals. Frequently people do not make it to the water for baptism before they receive the Holy Ghost.

I well remember a lady who consistently resisted all our attempts to get her to commit her life to Christ. She came to church several times but was turned off by the preaching of the Word of God. She argued at home with her husband and was the cause of much division in the home. Some six months previously he had come to the

Lord and was very happy that the love of God permeated his heart. His wife's disagreement with the truth kept him upset, but although perturbed, he steadfastly maintained his integrity with God. He often sought counsel lest he do something to hinder his companion. He kept praying, but seemingly to no avail. She seemed to become more resistant as time went by. He made many prayer requests at church services for the conversion of his wife.

God knows exactly how to handle each of us. On different occasions she met some of our people at work or in shopping centers. Each encounter drove conviction deeper in her heart. As she had a beautiful singing voice, her husband asked my wife to have her sing at a banquet. She was happy to do so. After the banquet many commented about her beautiful singing, and she was encouraged to attend the Sunday evening evangelistic service. Previously she seemed so hard and unmoved, but this night she came and found herself at the altar praying. Before she could even think about being baptized, she received the Holy Ghost. That night her faith went to work, and when it did, things happened fast.

Afterward in discussing her conversion, she stated that God had been dealing with her all the time she was resisting her husband. Although she put on a hard facade, his witnessing reached her. She tried to argue that this experience could not happen to people in this day and anyhow it wasn't for her. But little by little, she testified, the truth of God's Word sank in. The night she came to church and gave her heart to the Lord, she said, was a night of faith. She knew beyond a shadow of doubt that

God would meet her that night. Faith went to work, and when it did, things happened. God responds to faith.

"For she said within herself, If I may but touch his garment, I shall be whole" (Matthew 9:21).

Simple faith is all we need. There is nothing complicated about it. Often we make it that way, but it really is not. For example, there was a young lady who had prayed several times to receive the Holy Ghost after she came to the Lord and was baptized. A young man who had recently received the Holy Ghost saw her riding her bicycle across the university campus. He stopped and talked to her for a short time about receiving the Spirit. He told her it was not difficult and that God would give her the Holy Ghost just as He promised. All she needed was to have a sincere desire to receive and then to praise the Lord for the promise, and it would happen. As he had to go to another class he left. She looked out over the campus, her heart burning with a deep desire to pray, and spotted some trees a short distance away. Like the woman in the Bible who said, "If I can just touch the hem of His garment I shall be made whole." She said to herself, "I'll ride over to those trees and pray. Maybe I can receive the Holy Ghost."

She immediately put her faith into action and started riding. Miracle of miracles, she never made it to the trees.

She started to praise the Lord for the promise of the Holy Ghost as she rode, and she received the Spirit as she pedaled toward the trees. She put her faith to work, and things happened. They always do!

Faith overcomes every obstacle. The only thing that stood between the woman's determination and the Lord's garments was the thronging multitude. But faith pressed through. "If I can but touch . . ." she continued to say to herself, and that determination carried her through. The Lord responded the minute she touched His garment. The same is true of every one of us. We first believe, and at that very moment we start putting faith into action.

"Daughter, . . . thy faith hath made thee whole" (Matthew 9:22).

Faith is never passive. It motivates. It is not faith if it does not motivate us. Jesus proclaimed to the woman, "Daughter, . . . thy faith hath made thee whole." Although He was thronged by the crowd, He knew at once when she touched Him. He responds to active faith (Matthew 9:20).

A very important experience in my life will help illustrate what faith is and how we can appropriate it to receive God's response. Faith is a gift from God and comes through His Word.

I was in a hospital in Pensacola, Florida, with acute rheumatic fever. God had previously called me into the ministry, but because of a very unfortunate incident I had been very reluctant to commit myself fully to His will. Perhaps ignorance to His ways contributed to that reluctance. Later while on an evangelistic trip with another minister, I became ill and was admitted to the hospital.

The pain from this fever was extremely severe. The doctor told me I would be in the hospital about ten days, but now it was twenty-four days later, and I was worse than when I went in. I was paralyzed, lying in bed like a dead man in a casket. The drugs the doctor thought would soon take care of the fever had not worked, and I overheard the doctor tell my nurse that I had too much of it in my system. I had counted on its doing the work, but now it had to be taken away from me. I became very discouraged and felt there was no hope for me. In this downcast state of mind I turned to the Lord in sincere prayer—repenting for my reluctance to preach the gospel—and then promised if He would heal me, get me out of the hospital, I would go wherever He sent me. It was a big step. I would have to give up my farm; in fact, our livelihood would be in jeopardy.

Faith took over when I asked my wife to write one letter to my parents that we were leaving the farm and another letter to her sister and brother-in-law to move into our house and push our furniture into the front room. When we returned home, we would sell out to them.

At that point I was suffering as severely as any time during my illness. The letters were an act of faith. That is when faith really went to work. But it worked. The next morning I was a healed man! God moved during the night and took care of the terrible pain. It is now fifty-three years later, and that pain has never bothered me again. Faith works, but only when it is active!

In the previous chapters we established two important facts. (1) God has promised the Holy Ghost to every believer. (2) The crucifixion and resurrection of the Lord Jesus Christ has bridged the barrier of sin.

Now we come to the most important part of your coming to God. Do you believe that Jesus Christ died for your sins, was buried, and arose from the dead? Have you repented of your sins? Do you, right now, turn to God with all your heart? If so, and if you have not already received the Holy Ghost, you should be receiving without delay!

There need be no begging. To beg and plead is the language of unbelief. *Praise is the language of faith!* When we really believe, praise comes automatically from our hearts to God. It is not merely the words on our lips, but when praise comes from the heart it finds expression on the lips. It is not the abundance of the words that is important, but the fervency of faith with which we speak. When we truly become thankful for the provision of God, gratitude will come from the depths of our souls and reach the portals of glory. There will be a response. All the demons of hell cannot hold it back.

Real, genuine faith moves us toward God and God toward us!

CHAPTER FOUR

Waiting for the Promise

Waiting is one of the most difficult tasks for us "hurry-hurry" Americans. We want action! We get very impatient if things do not happen when we want them to. But wait we must.

There is no specific waiting period for a believer today as there was prior to Pentecost. There was a time element before, but not since. God decreed that the pouring out of the Holy Ghost would come on the day Israel commemorated the giving of the law. No one could have received the Holy Ghost before that day. Since then there is no restricted or specific time to receive.

The disciples could have done nothing to change the way God planned it. They prepared themselves, however, even though they did not know when it would happen.

What did they do to prepare themselves? Although these exact conditions will never occur again, it is good to learn from their experience. It gives us insight on how to wait effectively, although the Holy Ghost is available at any moment. The only waiting that we must do is conditioned entirely upon our ability to believe to the extent of unconditional surrender to Him!

We can learn a good lesson by observing what they did in those ten days of waiting. According to Luke 24:50-53, they returned to Jerusalem with great joy and were continually in the Temple, praising and blessing God.

They set themselves apart from society, left their occupations, spent their time in the Temple and the upper room—all of this with great joy flooding their souls as they continued praising and worshiping God. Although they could not have received until the ten days were up, they allowed themselves to become wholly occupied with the promise of God. That is a clue for anyone who desires to receive the Holy Ghost.

You must not allow any distractions. Keep the promise in mind; keep worshiping and praising Him with joy bells ringing in your heart. You do not have to give up your job, leave home, or anything like that. You must simply keep your mind on the Lord and His promises.

Why praise? It is the language of faith. Begging and pleading is the language of unbelief. When we really believe, we express that faith through the channel of praise. It is not mere words, but the expression of an attitude that grips a person. When praise comes from the heart it is a sure sign that faith is prompting it.

The apostle Paul beautifully illustrated this truth by the story of Abraham. God spoke to him that he was to have a son in his old age. Although he had his moments of doubt, he never mistrusted God or ascribed unfaithfulness to Him. Paul wrote about him, "And being not weak in faith, he considered not his own body now dead, when he was about an hundred years old, neither yet the deadness of Sarah's womb: he staggered not at the promise of God through unbelief; but was strong in faith, giving glory to God; and being fully persuaded that, what he had promised, he was able also to perform" (Romans 4:19-21).

"He staggered not at the promise of God through unbelief" (Romans 4:20).

When we study the life of Abraham, we find him erring on several occasions. These incidents reveal that he was truly human, enabling us to identify with him. He fully believed God's promise of a son—but he did waver in his confidence of how he was to come. His impatience gives us an important lesson in waiting. He believed the promise, but he could not wait. Waiting was the most difficult part of the whole ordeal. He allowed himself to take a detour from the path, by having a son by Hagar instead of Sarah—and he paid a tremendous price for this substitute way.

Even yet today the world is reeling with the results of that detour. Abraham never doubted the promise—but could not stand the waiting process.

Were there ever any waiting periods after Pentecost, and if so, how do we account for them?

The answer is yes! There are conditions at times that

we must not overlook. If someone does not receive the Holy Ghost, he should attempt to find out why.

There are three accounts of the Holy Ghost being delayed after faith began its work in hearts. One stands near the beginning of the church age; the other two were conditioned upon a lack of knowledge, which of course, is the fountainhead of faith. (See Romans 10:14, 17.)

The first account is in Acts 8. Jesus had given Peter the keys to the kingdom. (See Matthew 16:19.) He was God's man to open the door to the Jews in Judea, to the Samaritans, and to the Gentiles from the uttermost parts of the earth. (See Acts 1:8.) Peter was not present when the gospel was first preached to the Samaritans as he was at Pentecost and the house of the Gentile, Cornelius, where he was the spokesman with the keys. The Holy Ghost did not fall on the Samaritans until the apostles at Jerusalem sent Peter and John to them. When they arrived they immediately prayed for the Samaritans who had been baptized, and they received the Holy Ghost. (See Acts 8:15-17.) The presence and authority of these apostles inspired faith for the Samaritans to receive the promise, and Peter's role as spokesman was fulfilled in God's plan.

The other two events are the conversions of Saul of Tarsus and the Ephesian believers. (See Acts 9 and 19.) It is not difficult to discover at either place why the Holy Ghost was not poured out at once. Saul did not know. He had been told by the Lord that one Ananias would instruct him what he was to do. The first instructions he received when Ananias arrived three days later were to be baptized in the name of Jesus Christ and receive the Holy Ghost. There is no doubt the Lord could have filled him with the Holy Ghost on the Damascus Road, but he was not ready to receive, for he did not know to seek the Holy Ghost baptism. Knowledge is the forerunner of faith, and one must believe to receive.

In light of this account, it is surprising that so many modern churches are silent on the Holy Ghost experience, for Ananias included it in his first instructions to Saul. Jesus told Saul that Ananias would tell him what he must do, so receiving the Holy Ghost is clearly a necessary step. A great percentage of the church world is derelict in obeying Christ's commission by not teaching this experience.

"Have ye received the Holy Ghost since ye believed?" (Acts 19:2).

The final account is similar. Paul found believers at Ephesus and questioned them about their experience: "He said unto them, Have ye received the Holy Ghost since ye believed? And they said unto him, We have not so much as heard whether there be any Holy Ghost" (Acts 19:2). When he discovered their lack of knowledge about the Holy Ghost, he immediately instructed them so that they too could receive.

Are waiting periods necessary? Only if proper instructions have not been given. A person will not receive until

51

he has some knowledge that motivates him to seek.

The purpose of this booklet is to help alleviate this condition in a person's life. The Word of God brings light, and when correctly explained, that light will focus on the promise of God and inspire faith in a hungry heart.

Often we Pentecostals must be faulted for our lack of instruction on this important subject. Ananias took time with Saul, and he in turn took time to explain God's plan to the Ephesian believers.

"But seek ye first the kingdom of God, and his righteousness" (Matthew 6:33).

Chapter 1 has already explained that it certainly is scriptural to seek the Lord. The Lord made several statements to encourage people in this direction. In the Sermon on the Mount He stated, "Blessed are they which do hunger and thirst after righteousness: for they shall be filled. . . . But seek ye first the kingdom of God, and his righteousness; and all these things shall be added unto you" (Matthew 5:6: 6:33). After His resurrection He instructed His disciples to tarry at Jerusalem until they received power from on high (Luke 24:49).

He meant for them simply to wait until the promise came. He also meant that until they were equipped with the correct spiritual tools they should not try to do something they were not qualified to do. Yes, Jesus meant this and far more. As we see from Luke 24:49-53 and Acts 1:13-14, the believers did several things as they tarried:

1. They waited in the Temple at Jerusalem.

2. They were there *continually*—they stayed with it.

3. They praised and blessed God.

4. They "continued with one accord in prayer and supplication." They were together in their desire and intent, praying as they waited for the promise.

In short, Jesus instructed them about the promise. Having received His instructions, they praised and blessed God with great joy until the Spirit came.

From this account we learn the following sequence:

1. Receive instruction.

2. Set one's mind on the promise.

3. Wait, and while waiting praise and bless God until the promise comes.

4. When the person is ready, the filling will come immediately.

5. Often as one is praying, some unfinished business comes to mind, and it needs to be taken care of. For example, the apostles chose Matthias to replace Judas as they waited for the outpouring of the Spirit.

Unfinished Business

Once, my brother-in-law took a mink out of someone's trap one night as we were 'coon hunting. At the time he was not saved, and when I objected he laughed at me. Several years later he was praying, asking God to fill him with the Holy Ghost, and this incident came to mind.

He arose from prayer, came to me, and asked, "Fred, do you remember when I took that mink out of that trap several years ago while we were hunting?"

"Yes," I replied.

"I have to find whose trap that was and pay him the price of that mink hide," he solemnly stated.

He tried diligently to find the person who owned that trap but could not. So he asked me, "What shall I do? I can't pray with this hanging over my head."

"I know what I'd do," I replied.

"What?" he asked.

"I'd take the amount you received for the hide and put it in the offering at church," I answered.

He did so at the next service and was soon filled with the Holy Ghost. Yes, he had some unfinished business to take care of. It bothered him, and when he took care of it his faith was released and he received.

Unfinished business has caused many to fail to receive God's promise until they take care of it. If some unfinished business comes to you in prayer, take care of it at once.

Does such unfinished business hinder God from filling people with the Holy Ghost? Not when they truly repent, but it disturbs their faith. People need unobstructed faith in God's promises in order to receive. A clear conscience opens the door to unobstructed faith.

CHAPTER FIVE

What Will Happen?

The presence of God is awesome!

If you have never known or been surrounded by His presence, you are in for a fabulous experience when you receive the Holy Ghost! It is difficult, almost impossible, to explain. As one person affirmed, "It's better felt than 'telt.'" A glory enfolds you, envelopes you, and only when the experience is over do you suddenly realize that you have been overwhelmed with something from another world. It is God's glory, His magnificent presence! When His presence surrounds you, you may not know exactly what it is, but you know when it is. David extolled, "Thou wilt shew me the path of life: in thy presence is fulness of joy; at thy right hand there are pleasures for evermore" (Psalm 16:11).

When Moses first left Egypt, he did not know God was leading him. He had never basked in the glory of God. He was a stranger to it. Often he may have wondered why he left the splendor of Egypt to end up on the backside of a desert tending sheep. Nothing of any great consequence had happened to him until "by faith Moses, when he was come to years, refused to be called the son of Pharaoh's daughter; choosing rather to suffer affliction with the people of God, than to enjoy the pleasures of sin for a season" (Hebrews 11:24-25).

"Choosing rather to suffer affliction with the people of God, than to enjoy the pleasures of sin for a season" (Hebrews 11:25).

For forty years he waited and wondered. Then one day as he tended sheep, he espied a strange and unusual sight. A bush was burning but was not being consumed. Curious, he approached to investigate. He took only a few steps toward it when suddenly a commanding voice spoke to him. He stopped dead in his tracks when ordered, "Draw not nigh hither: put off thy shoes from off thy feet, for the place whereon thou standest is holy ground" (Exodus 3:5).

Moses had inadvertently walked into the imposing presence of God Almighty. It was an event that he would never forget nor stray from. It was a life-changing occurrence. His whole future came into sharp focus as he heard specific instructions from the One whose name He declared to be "I AM THAT I AM" (Exodus 3:14). Moses was in the glorious presence of the eternal God!

When Jesus' apostles heard Him pray as the morning

dawned across the Kidron Valley, they knew they were in the presence of the Almighty. Although they had been with Him for three and a half years, never before had they experienced such a hallowed moment as this, being over-whelmed by His awesome presence. It was a moment they would never forget. Although they did not know it, they were spending their last moments with Him in His earth-ly tabernacle. Their next communication with Him would occur after His resurrection.

His presence was striking, especially after His prayer in the Garden. When the band of men who came with Judas to take Him heard His words, "I am he," they imme-diately sprawled backward, falling to the ground humili-atingly entangled with one another. They were startled and wondering, "What is this?" His presence was then, and still is, awesome!

The two men on the Emmaus road, as Jesus left the table in their home, said, "Did not our hearts burn within us while he talked with us by the way?" (Luke 24:33).

The presence of God is a supreme experience in a person's life!

The Will of the Spirit to Occupy

As already noted, God has made many promises rela-tive to the baptism of the Holy Ghost. He is ready at any moment to fill us. There is no waiting period now as there was before the Day of Pentecost. The time and the place is up to us. If we believe, we shall receive. Baptizing is God's part; receiving is our part! God is not willing for anyone to perish; He wants all to come to repentance (II Peter 3:9).

A penitent attitude puts one on the receiving ground.

He is waiting on you!

The Struggle of Resistance

Paul explained to the Galatians, "For the flesh lusteth against the Spirit, and the Spirit against the flesh: and these are contrary the one to the other: so that ye cannot do the things that ye would" (Galatians 5:17).

The struggle starts even before we come to God. Whenever the Spirit begins dealing with us, immediately the resistance starts. Reasons by the dozen loom up in our mind, reasons why we should not take that step. But we must remember that the Spirit of God is striving, calling us to Him. At every turn a new degree of resistance appears, placed there, no doubt, by Satan. He does not want to give us up and will fight to the finish.

The very fact that there is a struggle should encourage us that we are on the right track. No resistance translates into no progress. As one writer said, "You can always tell when you're on the road to righteousness. . . . It's uphill!" When I sought for the Holy Ghost it seemed I would win one battle only to face another one immediately, but I persevered until victory came.

If you are having such a struggle, reinforce your faith by rereading the first chapter of this book. The many passages of Scripture it contains teach that the baptism of the Holy Ghost is for you.

The Breakthrough to Victory

The moment of receiving shall come, must come,

when we become thoroughly convinced that we need to seek Him with all our heart and soul. Time is of no great importance once we have reached that place. And we must remember that God is available all the time; it is simply a matter of yielding and receiving.

"Know ye not, that to whom ye yield yourselves servants to obey, his servants ye are to whom ye obey?" (Romans 6:16).

Paul stated, "Know ye not, that to whom ye yield yourselves servants to obey, his servants ye are to whom ye obey; whether of sin unto death, or of obedience unto righteousness? But God be thanked, that ye were the servants of sin, but ye have obeyed from the heart that form of doctrine which was delivered you. Being then made free from sin, ye became the servants of righteousness. I speak after the manner of men because of the infirmity of your flesh: for as ye have yielded your members servants to uncleanness and to iniquity unto iniquity; even so now yield your members servants to righteousness unto holiness" (Romans 6:16-19). In the same way that we once gave ourselves to evil, we must now yield ourselves to God in the same measure.

The condition of the 120 disciples on the Day of Pentecost should be the norm for all seekers: "And when the day of Pentecost was fully come, they were all with one accord in one place" (Acts 2:1).

Since they did not know how or when the Spirit would come, they focused their attention on Him, waiting in one accord. To be in one accord means to be in agreement. It is just that simple! We must set our minds on Christ, believe the promise, and do what they did: "And they worshipped him, and returned to Jerusalem with great joy: and were continually in the temple, praising and blessing God" (Luke 24:52-53).

They were at the right place with the right attitude at the right time! The place was the Temple; the attitude was one accord in faith, obedience, and yieldedness—all of this with staunch expressions of joy in their hearts. Then it happened!

It will happen to you too! Believe it and praise Him for the promise. You will break through to glorious victory!

God Takes Control

Paul stated in Romans 6:17-19 that we should yield our members to God. The most unruly member of our body is not our heart, mind, or hands, but rather our tongue.

"Behold, we put bits in the horses' mouths, that they may obey us; and we turn about their whole body. Behold also the ships, which though they be so great, and are driven of fierce winds, yet are they turned about with a very small helm, whithersoever the governor listeth. Even so the tongue is a little member, and boasteth great things. Behold, how great a matter

a little fire kindleth! And the tongue is a fire, a world of iniquity: so is the tongue among our members, that it defileth the whole body, and setteth on fire the course of nature; and it is set on fire of hell. For every kind of beasts, and of birds, and of serpents, and of things in the sea, is tamed, and hath been tamed of mankind: But the tongue can no man tame; it is an unruly evil, full of deadly poison" (James 3:3-8).

Since the tongue is so unruly and capable of causing so much trouble, it needs to be conquered, brought under control, and yielded to God. That is why God controls it as we receive the Holy Ghost. Whenever we yield that unruly, evil, poison-filled tongue to God, He takes over!

When the Lord begins to take over our tongue, we must let it go. With speaking in tongues comes an assurance, a confidence that we are now being baptized in and sealed with the Holy Spirit of promise. We now have the earnest of His inheritance within us, making us a vital part of His purchased possession (Ephesians 1:14). We have become one with the apostolic band and all of God's people.

The accounts in the Bible of speaking in tongues are not there just to fill up space. There is divine purpose in everything God does, and speaking in tongues is no exception. Some say it is an experience of the past that is no longer necessary, and some even say it is of the devil. They say they believe the Bible, yet refuse to accept speaking in tongues as being of God. Should we listen to such teaching in light of scriptural facts?

Our experience with God, coupled with the facts presented in the Word of God, should be sufficient to settle our mind about this most important element of salvation. The ultimate purpose for Jesus Christ's death was to impart new life to us by His Spirit. Without this experience in our Christian life we are devoid of one of the two purposes John the Baptist stated for Christ's coming into the realm of humanity:

• "The next day John seeth Jesus coming unto him, and saith, Behold the Lamb of God, which taketh away the sin of the world" (John 1:29).

• "And I knew him not: but he that sent me to baptize with water, the same said unto me, Upon whom thou shalt see the Spirit descending, and remaining on him, the same is he which baptizeth with the Holy Ghost" (John 1:33).

"The same is he which baptizeth with the Holy Ghost" (John 1:33).

John promised cleansing and filling. That is what Jesus came to do!

When these works take place in our lives, we become a part of God's wonderful church. We are ready to launch into a realm of God that will sustain us for the rest of our lives.

So many people, when they receive the Holy Ghost, think they have reached the ultimate in God. Although that may be true in a sense, there is much more to living, maturing, and working for Him. We cannot afford to be at ease in our newfound walk with God.

CHAPTER SIX

Life in the Spirit

Upon receiving the Holy Ghost we are launched into a new dimension in God. We are no longer just ordinary people on the streets. We have been transformed. We have become a new creation in Christ, ready to be trained in the things of God.

The Bible tells us, "All scripture is given by inspiration of God, and is profitable for doctrine, for reproof, for correction, for instruction in righteousness: that the man of God may be perfect, throughly furnished unto all good works" (II Timothy 3:16-17). The implication is that we should give ourselves to learning everything about the Word of God that we possibly can. Doing so is imperative. Several measures are necessary for our spiritual survival and growth, and this is one of them.

Communion with God

Two powerful forces are available to us that we should exercise immediately upon receiving the Holy Ghost. They are prayer and the study of the Word of God. These two factors are essential to our future. We are on a life-time journey. We will not plumb the depths of prayer or the Bible in a short time, but we should diligently pursue both. They should be among the greatest joys of our new Christian life. Communion with God should be voluntary, never a duty to perform.

A set time every day for these two items is the ideal. Early in the morning, if possible, is a good time, but if that is impractical, pick the time most suitable for you.

When my wife and I first came to the Lord we were farmers. I made it a habit to rise early each morning for prayer and study. They made a significant contribution to my life. Often I could scarcely wait for those wonderful moments with God. He communicated with me through His Word and spiritual blessings, and I responded to Him in sincere prayer and praise. Those times became the foundation of my spiritual life and have stood me in good stead throughout these sixty years. After this time of devotion, I would go about my work the rest of the day with a song in my heart and a continual praise on my lips. Usually the praises flowed all day long.

Make Bible reading, study, prayer and praise an every-day affair. Never allow it to become routine, as a duty to be performed. If it reaches that stage, it should be cause for alarm!

Joy in the Lord!

Paul gave this admonition about spiritual matters: "And be not drunk with wine, wherein is excess; but be filled with the Spirit. Speaking to yourselves in psalms and hymns and spiritual songs, singing and making melody in your heart to the Lord" (Ephesians 5:18-19).

To the Colossians he penned: "Let the word of Christ dwell in you richly in all wisdom; teaching and admonishing one another in psalms and hymns and spiritual songs, singing with grace in your hearts to the Lord" (Colossians 3:16).

"Let the word of Christ dwell in you richly in all wisdom" (Colossians 3:16).

One of the most faithful and influential men in our church works in a hospital. He sings and whistles hymns as he works. It attracts attention, but he does not do it for that reason. He is happy and joyful. Folks sense he is happy by his demeanor. Many ask, "Why are you so joyful?" He witnesses about what Jesus has done for him, and he also talks about the church. What better means of witnessing could a person develop? When we allow joy to emanate from our lives, people will be asking that question of us!

Sincere joy is an attribute to cherish. The writer of Hebrews stated, "By him therefore let us offer the sacrifice of praise to God continually, that is, the fruit of our lips giving thanks to his name" (Hebrews 13:15).

So let us be happy in the Lord and allow the praises to roll. Nehemiah 8:10 states so clearly that "the joy of the

LORD is your strength."

Jesus taught His disciples before His crucifixion that "my joy might remain in you, and that your joy might be full" (John 15:11). Joyfulness should emanate from a Christian like rays from the sun. The world can stand a lot of joyful Christians. They are searching for that type of Christianity. So let us be that!

We should not be joyful only on special occasions, spasmodically, but joy should be a part of our everyday life, even when things go wrong. James 1:2 admonishes, "Count it all joy when ye fall into divers temptations." It is the difficulty a person faces that strengthens his faith and resolve.

Coping with Problems

Problems are everywhere! Everybody has them. They come from both within and without. We have to cope with them wherever they are.

We have a new helper in the Spirit. Parents help their children when they confront a difficulty. They listen to their story, and do their best to provide a solution. God is no less interested in His children than we are in ours. We must count on His help. Here is how we can do so:

• "Be careful for nothing; but in every thing by prayer and supplication with thanksgiving let your requests be made known unto God. . . . I can do all things through Christ which strengtheneth me" (Philippians 4:6, 13).

• "And God is able to make all grace abound toward you; that ye, always having all sufficiency in all things, may abound to every good work" (II Corinthians 9:8).

• "Let your conversation be without covetousness; and be content with such things as ye have: for he hath said, I will never leave thee, nor forsake thee. So that we may boldly say, The Lord is my helper, and I will not fear what man shall do unto me" (Hebrews 13:5-6).

It is evident that God is vitally interested in each of us individually, not only to keep us and stand by our side (Matthew 28:20), but also to accomplish His designs in, through, and for us. He enables, empowers, strengthens, fortifies, qualifies, and authorizes us to do His will.

Do it!

CHAPTER SEVEN

A Church Home

Every Christian needs a church home? Indeed! Absolutely! Without question!

If for one moment you think you can make it by yourself, forget it. No one is strong enough to go it alone. Many have tried, only to end in disaster.

God established churches for specific reasons:

1. The need to belong
2. The need for fellowship
3. The need for the guidance of a leader
4. The need for someone to be responsible to
5. The need for a place to worship
6. The need for a place to contribute
7. The need for help
8. The need to be helpful

The Need to Belong

To belong means to have a close or friendly relationship to someone or to a group. In the case of the church, it is a matter of being closely involved with people of like faith. Young people especially feel this need. They love to be with their peers. They need to feel secure and wanted. Without this sense of belonging, a person feels left out, deprived, at a disadvantage, alone, and deserted.

To belong puts us in touch with the past, present, and future. We learn what has happened in the past, which gives us a proper perspective on the present and a vision for the future. To know what is happening today gives us a sense of being able to contribute to it or subtract from it. It gives us a feeling of having some influence. It also puts us in touch with future plans, making us knowledgeable of what we may be able to contribute to them.

The Need for Fellowship

Fellowship is an essential factor to the continuity of a Christian life. Without it one can feel alone in the battle to maintain his Christian experience with God. Simply put, fellowship is fellows in the same ship! It is those of like precious faith who embrace the same goals, head in the same direction, become part and parcel of each other, and associate with the same purpose.

The story is told of a believer who planned to move to a distant town where there was no church of his faith. In conversation, his pastor warned him about leaving a thriving church to go out on his own. He curtly informed the pastor that he had been sufficiently taught in the faith and nothing would ever move him from it. (See Colossians 1:23.) As they were talking in front of a fireplace, the pastor stepped to it, pulled a red-hot coal off to the side of the fire, returned to his chair, and continued talking. After some time he called attention to the coal, noting that it was no longer red hot as when he pulled it out of the fire.

"Do you see what happened to that red-hot coal when it was pulled from the fire?" he asked.

"Yes," replied the man, "it is no longer hot."

"You can be sure that will happen to you when you leave the fellowship of the church family. You need the church and the church needs you. You'll soon cool down if you do not make some provision for fellowship."

Fellowship is one of the grandest aspects of the Christian life. Everyone needs it. Although there is the possibility for conflict between members, that possibility is not nearly as serious as the danger of being deprived of fellowship. Many churches have an area called a fellowship hall where socials are held, dinners served, games played, and so on. They have it because they recognize the value of their people having fellowship with one another.

The Need for the Guidance of a Leader

Regardless of one's IQ, he needs to be taught the essential doctrines of the Bible. He needs instruction in matters of holiness, communication with God, communication with his fellow man, his walk and talk, dress, and many other things pertaining to the Christian life. He needs to learn how to teach others. If he does not learn how to follow, he can never learn how to lead. He needs the counsel of one who has been on the way for a long time, learning how to avoid the pitfalls that Satan puts in everyone's way.

The Bible is a big Book, and no one masters it in a hurry. Learning the various doctrines are quite important, and like the Ethiopian eunuch, everyone needs someone to teach him. (See Acts 8:30-31.) We all need honest, sincere teachers who are consistent, faithful, and hold the truth in righteousness.

The Need for Responsibility

No one is sufficient within himself to make it on his own. All of us need someone to whom we are responsible, who has accepted the task of leadership. Often this area of church life is neglected. Someone needs to be accountable for us, and we need to be accountable to him. If we miss church he needs to know why. If we are sick, we should notify this person so that he knows what is wrong. He can suggest that the pastor come and pray for us. Or he may want to come himself. This may seem like a small thing, but it is necessary. Many a person fails God because he thinks no one cares about him. We need to cultivate a responsible friendship with our leader. Otherwise we could be forgotten and become a casualty.

The Need for a Place to Worship

Worshiping God is a privilege, and without it we will fail as Christians. It is a necessity! The New Testament records a form of the word "worship" seventy-three times; clearly it is vitally important.

William Jennings Bryan wrote that man is a religious being; the heart instinctively seeks for a God. "Whether he worships on the banks of the Ganges, prays with the face upturned to the sun, kneels toward Mecca or, regarding all space as a temple, communes with his heavenly Father according to the Christian creed, man is essentially devout."

Harvey F. Ammerman described the importance of worship to our lives:

> One of the acid tests of a Christian is his attitude toward his possessions. Someone has figured out that one of every four verses in the Gospels is related to this attitude. I think the emphasis can be condensed into a single phrase: "What we worship determines what we become." If we worship material possessions, we tend to grow more materialistic. If we worship self, we become more selfish still. That is why Christ continually endeavored to direct men's worship.

Another writer, Lawrence R. Axelson, stated, "Worship is to Christian living what the mainspring is to a watch."

Humans need a place to worship, and that makes the church vitally important to us. We must go to a church that preaches the truth as recorded here and stay there as long as the pastor preaches this truth. We must not become a gadabout, running from church to church; doing so will rob us of credibility. Everyone needs to be found faithful!

The Need for a Place to Contribute

God wants the best we have. There is no way we will succeed by bringing the poorest of the flock, the lame, the blind, the sick, or the blemished. God said to Israel in Malachi 1:6-14:

"A son honoureth his father, and a servant his master: if then I be a father, where is mine honour? and if I be a master, where is my fear? saith the LORD of hosts unto you, O priests, that despise my name. And ye say, Wherein have we despised thy name? Ye offer polluted bread upon mine altar; and ye say, Wherein have we polluted thee? In that ye say, The table of the LORD is contemptible.

"And if ye offer the blind for sacrifice, is it not evil? and if ye offer the lame and sick, is it not evil? offer it now unto thy governor; will he be pleased with thee, or accept thy person? saith the LORD of hosts. And now, I pray you, beseech God that he will be gracious unto us: this hath been by your means: will he regard your persons? saith the LORD of hosts.

"Who is there even among you that would shut the doors for nought? neither do ye kindle fire on mine altar for nought. I have no pleasure in you, saith the LORD of hosts, neither will I accept an offering at your hand. For from the rising of the sun even unto the going down of the same my name shall be great among the Gentiles; and in every place incense shall be offered unto my name, and a pure offering: for my name shall be great among the heathen, saith the LORD of hosts.

"But ye have profaned it, in that ye say, The table of the LORD is polluted; and the fruit thereof, even his meat, is contemptible. Ye said also, Behold, what a weariness is it! and ye have snuffed at it, saith the LORD of hosts; and ye brought that which was torn, and the lame, and the sick; thus ye brought an offering: should I accept this of your hand? saith the LORD. But cursed be the deceiver, which hath in his flock a male, and voweth, and sacrificeth unto the LORD a corrupt thing: for I am a great King, saith the LORD of hosts, and my name is dreadful among the heathen."

God was asking for the best they had. He would not allow them to get by with something that was not the choicest of the flock. They had the best, but they determined to keep it for themselves. This attitude God could not accept.

"And prove me now herewith" (Malachi 3:10).

Neither will He accept anything from us that is not our best. Later in Malachi the Lord challenged Israel to bring their tithe into the storehouse (the tithe being the first fruits of their labors), and with this command He gave them a promise that He would open the windows of heaven and pour them out a blessing that there would not be room enough to receive it. He said if they would do this He would rebuke the devourer for their sakes and would not destroy the fruits of their ground. (See Malachi 3:7-11.)

To contribute is to give of ourselves and our labors to the Lord, not as a sacrifice for our sins but as a matter of principle, honoring Him for His love that He so graciously bestowed upon us.

Where do we bestow these things? According to Malachi, we should bring them to the storehouse, which in our day is the place where we worship and are fed spiritually.

If we do not give, there will soon be no place for God to pour His blessings into us. Solomon said, "Honour the LORD with thy substance, and with the firstfruits of all thine increase: so shall thy barns be filled with plenty, and thy presses shall burst out with new wine. My son, despise not the chastening of the LORD; neither be weary of his correction" (Proverbs 3:9-11).

"There is that scattereth, and yet increaseth; and there is that withholdeth more than is meet, but it tendeth to poverty. The liberal soul shall be made fat: and he that watereth shall be watered also himself" (Proverbs 11:24-25).

No one could say it any better!

The Need for Help

Sooner or later every Christian needs help. We need a specific place and person to turn to when a problem occurs. Often a testimony in church will help us. It is not always the preacher who helps, although chances are, the chief source of help will come from the one whom God has placed over us in the Lord. The minister, although perhaps not skilled in all facets of human relations, will be able to meet our needs. At least he will have contacts where those needs can be met.

If a minister has been pastoring very long, he will probably be a lot more skilled than one might think. His dealing with people as a pastor bestows on him a broad education in human relations.

As a pastor, it always amazed me at the wisdom that seemed to be on the tip of my tongue. Quite often as a person walked out the door of my office, I would say to myself, "Where did that bit of wisdom come from? I never faced that problem before." But the answer would be there, and I soon learned that when it became necessary, God gave me special wisdom to meet the need. The same is probably true of most ministers. The needs may be spiritual, financial, marital, job-related, or social. In time of need, we should not hesitate to confer with our pastor; that is why he is there.

The Need to Be Helpful

Every Christian needs to help others. Helping others is one of the most necessary of human relationships. The person who bestows all of his attention on himself will find himself shrinking pitifully in spiritual matters. The following quotes emphasize this truth:

• "A person all wrapped up in himself makes a mighty small package."

• "Who brings sunshine into the life of another has sunshine of his own" (David Johnson).

• "The key people in the kingdom of heaven will be those who have unlocked their hearts to the needs of others on earth" (William Ward).

• "A leader can best improve the efficiency of his followers by improving himself."

• "The man who makes himself better makes everyone

he comes in contact with better as well."

If our interests embrace only ourselves, we will soon be consumed by them. We should reach out to others, help them, pray for them, and talk to them about Jesus and what He has done for us. As we give people a ride to church and give them a few dollars if they are in financial need, our actions of generosity and assistance will make us feel exceptionally good!

CHAPTER EIGHT

Why Did God Choose Tongues?

(Adapted from a Tract)

He was a deacon in a fashionable church, but he did not believe in the Pentecostal doctrine relative to the baptism of the Holy Ghost. Yet he had been exposed to it through members of his immediate family. One night, at the close of an evangelistic service in an Apostolic church, he went forward to pray and was overwhelmingly filled with the Holy Ghost. He spoke in other tongues fluently and was so inundated in the Spirit that even hours later he could not speak English. Definitely, this was a biblical experience accompanied not only with speaking in tongues but also with joy and peace in the Holy Ghost.

Millions have experienced this same baptism in the Spirit. Wherever this message is proclaimed concerning the baptism of the Holy Ghost, the question is asked, "Why did God choose speaking in tongues as the initial, physical evidence of the baptism of the Holy Ghost?" There may be many answers to this question, and I do not claim to know them all. Some are obvious, however, and should be considered. First, we must recognize the sovereignty of God.

The Sovereignty of God

God is not accountable to us for what He chooses to do. Isaiah asked, "Who hath directed the Spirit of the LORD, or being his counsellor hath taught him? With whom took he counsel, and who instructed him, and taught him in the path of judgment, and taught him knowledge, and shewed to him the way of understanding?" (Isaiah 40:13-14).

We have no license to question His ways or to dispute His actions. His purposes are supreme, His promises sure, His performances sane and sensible.

After reading the following passages of Scripture, anyone with a hungry heart and an open mind will realize that there is a decided connection between speaking with tongues and the baptism of the Holy Ghost:

"For with stammering lips and another tongue will he speak to this people" (Isaiah 28:11).

"And these signs shall follow them that believe; In my name shall they cast out devils; they shall speak with new tongues" (Mark 16:17).

"And they were all filled with the Holy Ghost, and began to speak with other tongues, as the Spirit gave them utterance" (Acts 2:4).

"For they heard them speak with tongues, and magnify God" (Acts 10:46).

"And it came to pass, that, while Apollos was at Corinth, Paul having passed through the upper coasts

came to Ephesus: and finding certain disciples, he said unto them, Have ye received the Holy Ghost since ye believed? And they said unto him, We have not so much as heard whether there be any Holy Ghost. And he said unto them, Unto what then were ye baptized? And they said, Unto John's baptism. Then said Paul, John verily baptized with the baptism of repentance, saying unto the people, that they should believe on him which should come after him, that is, on Christ Jesus. When they heard this, they were baptized in the name of the Lord Jesus. And when Paul had laid his hands upon them, the Holy Ghost came on them; and they spake with tongues, and prophesied. And all the men were about twelve" (Acts 19:1-7).

"For ye have not received the spirit of bondage again to fear; but ye have received the Spirit of adoption, whereby we cry, Abba, Father" (Romans 8:15).

"And because ye are sons, God hath sent forth the Spirit of his Son into your hearts, crying, Abba, Father" (Galatians 4:6).

Why did God choose blood as a basis for atonement? Why did God choose water as the element in baptism? Why did God choose gold as the overlaying metal for the Ark of the Covenant? Why did God choose stone as the material upon which to record the law of Moses? Why did God choose Jerusalem as the site for His Temple? Why did God choose dust out of which to form man? There is divine purpose and reason behind each choice. We may not understand it all, but we most certainly would never attempt to deny or disavow God's sovereign right to do as He pleases or to choose what He wishes.

An External Evidence

There is a second vital and important reason why God chose other tongues as the evidence of a person's receiving the Holy Ghost. It is an external, outward evidence. There are many evidences of the operation of the Spirit of God in a person's life. With some it is a matter of time before they are manifested, such as the fruit mentioned in Galatians 5:22-23: "But the fruit of the Spirit is love, joy, peace, longsuffering, gentleness, goodness, faith, meekness, temperance: against such there is no law."

These attributes follow in the wake of the Spirit baptism and are the results of it. The apostle Peter and the six who accompanied him to Caesarea knew that the Gentiles had received the Holy Ghost, not because of longsuffering, gentleness, meekness or temperance, but because they heard them speak with tongues and magnify God. The text specifically points to speaking in tongues as the evidence of knowing: "For they heard them speak with tongues, and magnify God" (Acts 10:46).

Speaking in tongues was an outward, external evidence, instantly observable and heard. Peace, joy, righteousness, and the fruit of the Spirit are the internal, inward action, the long-term result of the filling.

A Uniform Evidence

A third reason why God chose other tongues as the evidence is uniformity. Many who oppose this statement will quote I Corinthians 12:30 as the basis of their opposition: "Do all speak with tongues?" This verse describes, however, the gift of tongues in operation in the life of the church, such as a public utterance to the congregation to be interpreted. (See I Corinthians 12:10; 14:27-28.) Though both speaking in tongues as the evidence of the Spirit baptism and speaking in tongues as a gift to edify the church are the same in essence, they are different in administration and operation.

"Do all speak with tongues?" (I Corinthians 12:30).

The same thing is true of faith itself. To be saved, everyone must have a certain degree of faith. (See John 3:16; Romans 10:9; Ephesians 2:8). Yet there is also the gift of faith for special needs, which not everyone receives on a continual basis. (See I Corinthians 12:4-11.) The faith necessary for salvation and the gift of faith are the same in essence but different in administration and operation.

To demonstrate the contrast between speaking in tongues as the evidence of the Holy Ghost and the gift of tongues for corporate worship, we can compare the accounts in Acts with the instructions in I Corinthians. Speaking in tongues in Acts would be out of order if it were considered as the gift of tongues mentioned in I Corinthians 12:10. In I Corinthians 14:27-28, Paul gave instructions for the use of this gift: "If any man speak in an unknown tongue, let it be by two, or at the most by three, and that by course; and let one interpret. But if there be no interpreter, let him keep silence in the church; and let him speak to himself, and to God."

Those who operate the gift of tongues must speak by course and at the most only three messages. Yet on the Day of Pentecost, 120 spoke in tongues at once. At the household of Cornelius there were several speaking at the same time. Then, when Paul met the Ephesians, twelve men spoke in tongues at one time. Another instruction that would have been violated in all three of these incidents, if they were considered the gift of tongues, was the requirement that there be an interpretation.

"Likewise the Spirit also helpeth our infirmities" (Romans 8:26).

From this comparison and from a study of Acts and I Corinthians, we can easily determine the difference between the three operations of speaking in tongues: (1) the initial evidence of receiving the Holy Ghost, (2) the operation of the gift with an interpretation for the church, and (3) tongues for personal devotion and prayer.

As an example of the third use, if no interpretation is forthcoming in a church service, the person who speaks in tongues can still speak to himself and to God. Romans 8:26 apparently refers to this third use also: "Likewise the

Spirit also helpeth our infirmities: for we know not what we should pray for as we ought: but the Spirit itself maketh intercession for us with groanings which cannot be uttered."

In speaking about being born of the Spirit, Jesus stated in John 3:8, "The wind bloweth where it listeth, and thou hearest the sound thereof, but canst not tell whence it cometh, and whither it goeth: so is every one that is born of the Spirit."

Jesus spoke of uniformity in the experience of receiving the Spirit. We should note that Jesus placed emphasis upon the word "sound." We hear the wind blowing, and this sound is the evidence of its presence. Neither seeing nor feeling is of primary importance, although these evidences may be present, but hearing the sound is the most signficant.

Some may conclude that Jesus simply referred to the experience at Pentecost, when the believers heard the sound as of a rushing mighty wind. This rushing mighty wind, however, did not occur in Acts 10:46 or 19:6, but speaking in tongues did. Hence, we must conclude that the important aspect of the Spirit's evidence at Pentecost was speaking in tongues. *The wind was impersonal; the speaking in tongues was personal.*

At Caesarea all who heard the Word were filled:

"While Peter yet spake these words, the Holy Ghost fell on all them which heard the word. And they of the circumcision which believed were astonished, as many as came with Peter, because that on the Gentiles

87

also was poured out the gift of the Holy Ghost. For they heard them speak with tongues, and magnify God. Then answered Peter, Can any man forbid water, that these should not be baptized, which have received the Holy Ghost as well as we? And he commanded them to be baptized in the name of the Lord. Then prayed they him to tarry certain days" (Acts 10:44-48).

We should notice that all who heard the Word also spoke in tongues. The "them" of verse 46 is the same "them" in verse 44.

Likewise, all twelve mentioned in Acts 19:6 had a uniform experience:

"And when Paul had laid his hands upon them, the Holy Ghost came on them, and they spake with tongues, and prophesied."

If ten had received the Holy Ghost by speaking in tongues and two had not spoken in tongues, would Paul have accepted their experience? Surely not. They exhibited the same uniform evidence.

Complete Control

Speaking in tongues symbolizes God's complete control of the believer. Perhaps this is one of the most outstanding reasons why God chose speaking in tongues as the initial evidence of the Holy Ghost baptism. James gave more information about the tongue than any other writer in the New Testament. His teaching about the nature of the tongue is quite revealing:

"For in many things we offend all. If any man offend not in word, the same is a perfect man, and able also to bridle the whole body. Behold, we put bits in the horses' mouths, that they may obey us; and we turn about their whole body. Behold also the ships, which though they be so great, and are driven of fierce winds, yet are they turned about with a very small helm, whithersoever the governor listeth. Even so the tongue is a little member, and boasteth great things. Behold, how great a matter a little fire kindleth! And the tongue is a fire, a world of iniquity: so is the tongue among our members, that it defileth the whole body, and setteth on fire the course of nature; and it is set on fire of hell. For every kind of beasts, and of birds, and of serpents, and of things in the sea, is tamed, and hath been tamed of mankind: but the tongue can no man tame; it is an unruly evil, full of deadly poison. Therewith bless we God, even the Father; and therewith curse we men, which are made after the similitude of God. Out of the same mouth proceedeth blessing and cursing. My brethren, these things ought not so to be. Doth a fountain send forth at the same place sweet water and bitter? Can the fig tree, my brethren, bear olive berries? either a vine, figs? so can no fountain both yield salt water and fresh. Who is a wise man and endued with knowledge among you? let him shew out of a good conversation his works with meekness of wisdom" (James 3:2-13).

First, the tongue is capable of defiling the whole body. If it is capable of this action, is it incredible to claim that it is also capable of sanctifying the whole body? Second, though the tongue is a small member, it has never been tamed of mankind. It is the most unruly member of the body. If this be true about the tongue, would it not be necessary for it be tamed before the whole body could be consecrated to God? James illustrated the importance of the tongue by comparing it to the bit in a horse's mouth, which gives the driver complete control over the horse. Likewise, the helm of a large vessel gives the pilot full command of the ship. The implication is that whoever controls the tongue of a person, controls him.

The tongue takes on great importance when we understand these things. We cannot take care of it ourselves; only God can. In Matthew 12:29 Jesus stated that before someone can enter a strong man's house and spoil or plunder his goods, he must first bind the strong man. *The strong man of our house is our tongue.* We can tame every member of our body but this one. When God tames our tongue, we are under the control of the great God of the heavens. We are in the hands of Almighty God, conquered by Christ, and endued with a spiritual force from on high. Not only are we adopted into His body, but we are also empowered for His service.

Our Greatest Expression

The tongue is the greatest expression of the human spirit. We are spiritual creatures; we are emotional. Because we are emotional, we must give expression to our emotions. The ability and power to coordinate thought and tongue into intelligent speech is one of our highest abilities. It elevates us above the beasts of the field. It makes us superior to the rest of God's creation. It is the most distinguishing feature of our being. The tongue is the vehicle of expression for the spirit. All of our emotions—such as love, hate, anger, sorrow, joy, happiness, relief, and serenity—are communicated through the tongue. It is the gateway to our heart, feelings, spirit, and attitudes.

In light of these truths, it is not difficult to see why God would use speaking in tongues to express the greatest, most wonderful experience that mortal humans could receive. In the baptism of the Holy Ghost, His Spirit and ours become one. He uses our tongue and voice to express that unity. It is a wonder of wonders, chosen not by humans, but by God, the sovereign ruler of the universe.

Why should we be found fighting against Him? Let us believe His Word, accept what He says, and receive the baptism of the Holy Ghost. In Luke 11:13 Jesus assured us that God wants to give all of us this great experience:

"If ye then, being evil, know how to give good gifts unto your children: how much more shall your heavenly Father give the Holy Spirit to them that ask him?"

Conclusion

The Pentecostals did not invent speaking in tongues. God did!

The Pentecostals did not put speaking in tongues in the Bible. God did!

The Pentecostals did not first associate speaking in tongues with receiving the Holy Ghost. God did!

The Pentecostals did not promise the Spirit would come as the wind blowing, with our not knowing where it came from and where it was going but being able to hear its sound. God did!

The first Pentecostals on the Day of Pentecost did not ask to speak in tongues. God did it!

Did the apostle Peter err on the Day of Pentecost when he answered the cry of three thousand souls with the message of Acts 2:38? Certainly not!

Cornelius and his household knew nothing about the Holy Ghost and tongues, yet when the Holy Ghost came to them, so did speaking in tongues. They did not create the situation. God did!

When Paul found the Ephesian disciples and asked, "Did you receive the Holy Ghost when you believed?" they answered, "We did not know there was a Holy Ghost." He instructed them and then laid his hands on them. They received the Spirit and spoke in tongues. Did Paul give them the Holy Ghost? No, God did!

Who is so spiritual as to have the authority to say that

God did not mean for us to receive this experience today? Did God ever say that? No, He did not!

Have you received the Holy Ghost yet?

God has planned it for you!

About the Author

FRED KINZIE and his wife, Vera, after coming to the Lord were soon wholeheartedly involved in gospel work—in evangelism for almost ten years and then as pastor of a small church in Toledo, Ohio. Today a large congregation worships the Lord at the First Apostolic Church there. Both have been involved in official capacities in the United Pentecostal Church International: she as president of the Ladies Auxiliary Division and he as a member of the Foreign Missions Board. Since resigning as pastor of the First Apostolic Church, Toledo, Ohio, in 1983, Fred Kinzie has devoted himself to writing. Three books, *Strength through Struggle, Salvation in the Book of Acts* and *John: The Gospel that Had to Be Written,* have previously been published by Word Aflame Press. After sixty years in the Christian life and seeing multitudes receive the Holy Ghost, his desire with the writing of this new book, *Handbook on Receiving the Holy Ghost,* is to help bring hungry hearts to that wonderful pinnacle of Christian experience, the reception of the gift of the Holy Ghost.